The Seven Deadly Sins

The Seven Deadly Sins

A WICKED ANTHOLOGY OF WIT AND WISDOM

Compiled by Steve Dobell

PAVILION

First published in Great Britain in 1997 by
PAVILION BOOKS LIMITED
26 Upper Ground
London SE1 9PD

General introduction and chapter introductions © Steve Dobell 1997
Selection © Steve Dobell

Picture Acknowledgements
Cover, pages 23, 49 and 63 appear courtesy of Mary Evans Picture Library
Page 13 © Estate of H.M. Bateman
Page 85 © Punch Cartoon Library

Designed by Elizabeth Ayer

A CIP catalogue record for this book is available from the British Library

ISBN 1 86205 073 2

Printed and bound in Finland by WSOY

2 4 6 8 10 9 7 5 3 1

This book may be ordered by post direct from the publisher.
Please contact the Marketing Department. But try your bookshop first.

Contents

STEVE DOBELL grew up in Gloucestershire but now leads a relatively blameless life in south-west London. His acquaintance with sin, such as it is, stems from close links with the gritty underworld of the public library services and, in particular, the notorious London Library.

Also by Steve Dobell
DOWN THE PLUGHOLE
An irreverent history of the bath, from Minoan Crete to the present day.

'Charming and erudite' *Oxford Times*

'Ideal bathtime reading' *South Wales Argus*

'Bubbling with fun . . . it is a tribute to the author's sense of humour and scholarship that in 94 pages he never flags or repeats himself on the subject of the bath' *Aberdeen Evening Express*

Introduction

SIN is one of the most powerful and menacing words in the language. It still sends a frisson of pleasurable horror down the spine of the heathen and the God-fearing alike. While the idea of sin stems from religion – and the greater the fear of God, no doubt, the less pleasurable and more horrific that frisson feels – even for those without any fear of damnation it retains tremendous force.

The seven deadly sins – wrath, gluttony, avarice, lust, envy, pride and sloth – are a medieval concept. They had all been rife since the beginning of time, of course, and had featured in the literature of Ancient Greece and elsewhere. It was in the Middle Ages, however, and independently of the Church, that these seven were formally identified in the public mind as the ugliest and most hated sins, which could pervert the soul and destroy its owner's hopes of salvation.

In this more utilitarian age there is a tendency to be less concerned about our souls than about the effects of our actions on others. Violence, cruelty, malice and dishonesty are therefore seen as more harmful than the relatively private 'deadly' sins that so alarmed our ancestors. This is why gluttony, which only really affects the perpetrator, is not taken very seriously, whereas drunkenness is, as it is a frequent cause of accidents, brawls and domestic violence.

Nevertheless, while not all of the seven deadly sins have great horror value now, compared with violent crime in particular, they do all represent basic human frailties, passions or obsessions which in extreme cases can and do lead to criminal behaviour. They can therefore be seen, albeit unfashionably, as the roots of crime. Murders and other acts of violence usually derive from various forms of wrath or lust; others from avarice and envy, which are also responsible for most of the desperate and dishonest things done to obtain money or power. Not so many crimes, admittedly, stem from pride or gluttony, and fewest of all from sloth, which tends to put the kibosh on pretty well everything.

Most of the wise and witty things written or uttered about sin have indeed been on the subject of these very frailties and passions rather than on specific crimes. One would be hard pressed to fill a book with *bons mots* on murder, GBH, rape et al – and few would wish to read it in any case – while, for centuries past, philosophical generalizations on human imperfections have always been good for a bit of soul-searching – or a laugh. Gluttony and lust, in particular, have produced a remarkable quantity of entertaining writing, and therefore have longer chapters here than the other sins. The modern age has a relaxed attitude to this pair, and to sloth, while even envy and avarice, pride and wrath are treated leniently.

The people who do most to encourage leniency towards these sins – indeed to promote them – are of course advertisers. Or if they don't, it is not for want of trying. 'We understand you completely,' they constantly tell us. 'You want to make a lot of money fast and without effort; you want to keep up with the Joneses and get ahead of the Germans; you want to cut a more distinguished figure than your competitors and colleagues; you want to make your friends and neighbours green with envy – and you also want that dishy creature on the fourth floor. Just buy our product, use our service, take our advice, and you shall. All this will be yours. You'll be irresistible. It's OK, take the last one – take it off her plate.'

They know – or believe – that our only aim in life is to bask in luxury and eat luscious *bonnes bouches*, while enjoying more legroom and leaving the rest behind. 'Go on, pamper yourself,' is the message – to all and sundry – 'you deserve it.' One wonders how they know.

Trading on the sins of envy, avarice and pride, advertisers legitimize not only these but also gluttony, lust and sloth. The only deadly sin they seem to have overlooked is wrath. It can only be a matter of time, one might suppose, before this systematic Mephistophelian activity incurs wrath of the divine kind. However, one should not get carried away. Sin was around before advertising and, as the examples in this book will demonstrate, it can do very well without any help. (And God knows better than to interfere. That's why we like him.)

The quotations take the form of aphorisms, epigrams, *bons mots*, light verse, and extracts from novels, plays, poetry and song, as well as other sources. The tone, of course, varies widely. Many writers, especially the earlier ones, have been appalled by sin; some have offered advice on how to resist it; some have been content to portray the action of sins; others have refuted the very existence of a sin or laughed in its face. All these attitudes have found a welcome here. Nor is there a consistent guiding principle in the order of the quotations, except that satisfying juxtapositions have not been resisted. Thus writers of the same or completely different periods can sometimes be seen answering each other, putting a contrasting point of view or providing unexpected support. The result, I hope, is an enjoyable potpourri of thought-provoking contrasts and interesting alliances. What the selections have in common, wherever they come from, is that they were all intended, following the principle espoused by Geoffrey Chaucer (and his disciple Lord Reith), either to instruct or to entertain – or both. The only criterion for inclusion has been that they still do.

Wrath

Putting to sea in a storm

OF ALL the deadly sins, wrath is arguably the least revolting and objectionable. We all experience it and understand it, and sometimes, perhaps, are the better for it. There are those who claim that it is better to let it out than to bottle it up. It is less all-pervasive than other sins: the person who frequently gives way to wrath may be difficult to live with, but may also be a delight when not actually in its grip. It was not always viewed in this indulgent light, but from the word go we humans were in good company. While nations who give way to wrath now face the threat of nuclear war, for individuals and nations alike the ultimate sanction has always been the wrath of God.

Day of wrath! O day of mourning!
See fulfilled the prophets' warning,
Heaven and earth in ashes burning!

Tommaso di Celano, *Dies Irae*

He treadeth the winepress of the fierceness and wrath of Almighty God.

Revelation, XIX.15

Then Herod, when he saw that he was mocked of the wise men, was exceeding wroth, and sent forth, and slew all the children that were in Bethlehem, and in all the coasts thereof, from two years old and under, according to the time which he had diligently enquired of the wise men.

Matthew, II.16

Sudden passion is called short-lived madness; it is a madness indeed, but the fits of it return so often in choleric people that it may well be called a continual madness.

Lord Chesterfield, *Letters*

Every stroke our Fury strikes is sure to hit ourselves at last.

William Penn, *Some Fruits of Solitude*

To be angry, is to revenge the fault of others upon ourselves.

Alexander Pope, *Thoughts on Various Subjects*

Anger is a better sign of the heart than of the head; it is a breaking out of the disease of honesty.

Lord Halifax, *Moral Thoughts and Reflections*

Act nothing in furious Passion; it's putting to Sea in a Storm.

Dr Thomas Fuller, *Introductio ad Prudentiam*

You common cry of curs! whose breath I hate
As reek o' the rotten fens, whose loves I prize
As the dead carcases of unburied men
That do corrupt my air, I banish you;
And here remain with your uncertainty!
Let every feeble rumour shake your hearts!
Your enemies, with nodding of their plumes,
Fan you into despair! Have the power still
To banish your defenders; till at length
Your ignorance . . . deliver you as most
Abated captives to some nation
That won you without blows! Despising,
For you, the city, thus I turn my back:
There is a world elsewhere.

William Shakespeare, *Coriolanus*

When angry, count four; when very angry, swear.

Mark Twain, *Pudd'nhead Wilson*

The greatest remedy for anger is delay.

Seneca, *De Ira*

Anger raiseth Invention, but it overheateth the Oven.

Lord Halifax, *Works*

Observe a man in a passion, see his eyes glaring, his face enflamed, his limbs trembling, and his tongue stammering and faltering with rage, and then ask yourself calmly whether upon any account you would be that human wild-beast.

Lord Chesterfield, *Letters*

Those who are at war with others, are not at peace with themselves. It is the uneasiness, the turbulence, the acrimony within that recoils upon external objects.

William Hazlitt, *Criticisms on Art*

A man who can't control his temper is like a city without defences.

Jewish proverb

Be ye angry, and sin not: let not the sun go down upon your wrath.

Ephesians, IV.26

You heavens, give me that patience, patience I need!
You see me here, you gods, a poor old man,
As full of grief as age; wretched in both!
If it be you that stir these daughters' hearts
Against their father, fool me not so much
To bear it tamely; touch me with noble anger,

And let not women's weapons, water-drops,
Stain my man's cheeks! No, you unnatural hags,
I will have such revenges on you both
That all the world shall – I will do such things –
What they are yet I know not – but they shall be
The terrors of the earth. You think I'll weep;
No, I'll not weep:
I have full cause of weeping, but this heart
Shall break into a hundred thousand flaws
Or ere I'll weep. O fool! I shall go mad.

William Shakespeare, *King Lear*

How much more grievous are the consequences of anger than
the causes of it.

Marcus Aurelius, *Meditations*

Be particularly watchful against heat of temper; it makes constant work for repentance and chagrine.

Eliza Pinckney, *Journal and Letters*

Burning with the fires of hatred, the more they gnaw others,
spewing forth words, the more are they wordless, gnawed
within.

Laura Cereta, *Epistolae*

Heaven has no rage like love to hatred turned,
Nor hell a fury like a woman scorned.

William Congreve, *The Mourning Bride*

When we debate our trivial difference loud,
We do commit murder in healing wounds.

William Shakespeare, *Antony and Cleopatra*

I am righteously indignant; *you* are annoyed; *he* is making a fuss
about nothing.

New Statesman competition entry

' – if I had him here. If I only had him here –'

'Oh Quilp!' said his wife, 'what's the matter? Who are you
angry with?'

' – I should drown him,' said the dwarf, not heeding her. 'Too
easy a death, too short, too quick – but the river runs close at
hand. Oh! if I had him here! Just to take him to the brink,
coaxingly and pleasantly, – holding him by the button-hole –
joking with him, – and, with a sudden push, to send him splash-
ing down! Drowning men come to the surface three times, they
say. Ah! To see him those three times, and mock him as his face
came bobbing up, – oh, what a rich treat that would be!'

Charles Dickens, *The Old Curiosity Shop*

Anger and jealousy can no more bear to lose sight of their objects than love.

George Eliot, *The Mill on the Floss*

A gentle answer turns away wrath; but harsh words stir up anger.

Book of Proverbs

I was angry with my friend;
I told my wrath, my wrath did end.
I was angry with my foe;
I told it not, my wrath did grow.

William Blake, 'A Poison Tree'

His figure was pleasing and majestic; but when he was angry one of his eyes became so terrible that no person could bear to behold it, and the wretch upon whom it was fixed instantly fell backward, and sometimes expired. For fear, however, of depopulating his dominions, and making his palace desolate, he but rarely gave way to his anger.

William Beckford, *Vathek*

Ah, if I were not king, I should lose my temper.

Louis XIV

It's my rule never to lose me temper till it would be detrimental to keep it.

Sean O'Casey, *The Plough and the Stars*

Every normal man must be tempted, at times, to spit on his hands, hoist the black flag, and begin slitting throats.

H.L. Mencken, *Prejudices*

Anybody can become angry – that is easy; but to be angry with the right person, and to the right degree, and at the right time, and for the right purpose, and in the right way – that is not within everybody's power and is not easy.

Aristotle, *Nicomachean Ethics*

The tigers of wrath are wiser than the horses of instruction.

William Blake, 'Proverbs of Hell'

As we jog on, either laugh with me, or at me, or in short do anything, – only keep your temper.

Laurence Sterne, *Tristram Shandy*

Gluttony

Our first distress

EATING an apple may not sound gluttonous, but if on one portentous occasion it was, then Chaucer has a point when he asserts that gluttony was in fact the original sin, just pipping lust for first place. Among all these more or less universal sins, gluttony is arguably the most widespread, and it is appropriate that here one of the greatest of all commentators on human fallibility, Dr Johnson, is also a prime exponent. Today, no doubt, he would be said to have an eating disorder.

Another kind of disorder is represented here. Since prodigious feats at the table imply prodigies in the kitchen, it seemed appropriate to include a piece that provides a glimpse of the aftermath behind the scenes. I have also taken gluttony to include large-scale drinking, as it seems to me that the two, though separate, go hand in hand, and if the one is a deadly sin, then the other must at least warrant a subsection.

More controversial, perhaps, is the question of cannibalism, which again seems to me to deserve a corner of this book, though it may not be gluttonous *per se*. How many persons a team of Melanesian cannibals of average weight, say, would need to consume to qualify them as gluttons is well beyond my competence to judge. Probably at least several of the top-order batsmen. The contribution by the late Willie Rushton, I therefore concede, may be out of court, as only a single victim, or dish, has been eaten by an unspecified number of opponents, but his account deserves a second innings, both as an authentic rendering of MCC loftiness and as a reminder of a very funny writer.

And the Lord God said unto the woman, What is this that thou hast done? And the woman said, The serpent beguiled me, and I did eat.

Genesis, III.13

O cursed gluttony, our first distress!
Cause of our first confusion, first temptation,
The very origin of our damnation,
Till Christ redeemed us with his blood again!
O infamous indulgence! Cursed stain
So dearly bought! And what has it been worth?
Gluttony has corrupted all the earth.

Geoffrey Chaucer, *The Pardoner's Tale*

There is no love sincerer than the love of food.

George Bernard Shaw, *Man and Superman*

Glutton, *n*. A person who escapes the evils of moderation by committing dyspepsia.

Ambrose Bierce, *The Devil's Dictionary*

They are as sick that surfeit with too much,
As they that starve with nothing.

William Shakespeare, *The Merchant of Venice*

My advice if you insist on slimming: Eat as much as you like –
just don't swallow it.

Harry Secombe, *Daily Herald*

They surfeited with honey and began
To loathe the taste of sweetness, whereof a little
More than a little is by much too much.

William Shakespeare, *Henry IV, Part I*

I eat merely to put food out of my mind.

N.F. Simpson, *The Hole*

Moderation is a fatal thing. Nothing succeeds like excess.

Oscar Wilde, *A Woman of No Importance*

I have not been afraid of excess: excess on occasion is
exhilarating. It prevents moderation from acquiring the
deadening effect of a habit.

W. Somerset Maugham, *The Summing Up*

Gluttony is an emotional escape, a sign that something is
eating us.

Peter de Vries, *Comfort Me with Apples*

No miserliness or gluttony is equal to Santra's. When he has
been invited and hurried off to the grand dinner which he has
for so many nights and days fished for, he asks thrice for
kernels of boar, four times for the loin, and for each leg of a
hare . . . and when his napkin is already bursting under his
thousand thefts, he secretes, in the reeking folds of his gown,
gnawed vertebrae . . .

Martial, *Epigrams*

I am an epicure; *you* are a gourmand; *he* has both feet in the
trough.

New Statesman competition entry

I never knew any man who relished good eating more than he
did. When at table, he was totally absorbed in the business of
the moment; his looks seemed riveted to his plate; nor would he,
unless when in very high company, say one word, or even pay
the least attention to what was said by others, till he had
satisfied his appetite, which was so fierce, and indulged with
such intenseness, that while in the act of eating, the veins of his
forehead swelled, and generally a strong perspiration was
visible. To those whose sensations were delicate, this could not
but be disgusting; and it was doubtless not very suitable to the
character of a philosopher, who should be distinguished by
self-command. But it must be owned, that Johnson, though he
could be rigidly *abstemious*, was not a *temperate* man in eating or

drinking. He could refrain, but he could not use moderately. He told me, that he had fasted two days without inconvenience, and that he had never been hungry but once. They who beheld with wonder how much he ate upon all occasions when his dinner was to his taste, could not easily conceive what he must have meant by hunger . . .

James Boswell, *The Life of Samuel Johnson*

One should eat to live, and not live to eat.

Molière, *L'Avare*

They have digged their grave with their teeth.

Thomas Adams, *Works*

More die from overeating than from undereating.

Nachman of Bratslav

More are slain by suppers than the sword.

English proverb

I saw few die of hunger; of eating, a hundred thousand.

Benjamin Franklin, *Poor Richard*

I have heard it remarked by a statesman of high reputation, that most great men have died of over-eating themselves.

Henry Taylor, *Sermons*

Afterwards, satisfied that his duty was done, he made excuses to his neighbours and went off in search of the kitchens. These, a few yards from the banqueting hall, presented a scene of unspeakable chaos. It suggested to Bognor's food-and-drink-sated – and therefore impressionable – mind one of those immense oil paintings to be found in a French museum of a certain sort and entitled 'After Borodino'. The atmosphere was heavy with steam and cigarette smoke. There was debris every-where: bones and raw flesh and egg and oyster shells; blood and chocolate; cabbage leaves and broken brandy bottles. Among this men and women, many in tight check trousers, white jackets or aprons, sometimes a tall chef's hat, wandered about dazed, as if shell-shocked. Others sat on stools or chairs, or slumped over stoves and sinks. Some were asleep, some drinking, some smoking; in one corner a Franco-Japanese group had begun a poker school.

Tim Heald, *Just Desserts*

There is small danger of being starved in our land of plenty; but the danger of being stuffed is imminent.

Sarah Josepha Hale, *Traits of American Life*

The appetite comes with eating.

Rabelais, *Gargantua and Pantagruel*

Food is an important part of a balanced diet.

Fran Lebowitz, *Metropolitan Life*

We lived for days on nothing but food and water.

W.C. Fields

Drink! for you know not whence you came, nor why:
Drink! for you know not why you go, nor where.

Edward FitzGerald, *The Rubáiyát of Omar Khayyám*

Today it is our pleasure to be drunk;
And this our queen shall be as drunk as we.

Henry Fielding, *Tom Thumb the Great*

. . . Stated very simply it was this: Mr Rasselyer-Brown drank.

It was not meant that he was a drunkard or that he drank too much, or anything of that sort. He drank. That was all.

There was no excess about it. Mr Rasselyer-Brown, of course, began the day with an eye-opener – and after all, what alert man does not wish his eyes well open in the morning? He followed it usually just before breakfast with a bracer – and what wiser precaution can a business man take than to brace his breakfast? On his way to business he generally had his motor stopped at the Grand Palaver for a moment, if it was a raw day, and dropped in and took something to keep out the damp. If it was a cold day he took something to keep out the cold, and if it was one of those clear, sunny days that are so dangerous to the system he took whatever the bar-tender (a recognized health expert) suggested to tone the system up. After which he could sit down in his office and transact more business, and bigger business, in coal, charcoal, wood, pulp, pulp-wood, and wood-pulp, in two hours than any other man in the business could in a week. Naturally so. For he was braced, and propped, and toned up, and his eyes had been opened, and his brain cleared, till outside of very big business indeed few men were on a footing with him.

Stephen Leacock, *Arcadian Adventures with the Idle Rich*

After four martinis, my husband turns into a disgusting beast. And after the fifth, I pass out altogether.

Anon.

Abstainer, *n.* A weak person who yields to the temptation of denying himself a pleasure.

Ambrose Bierce, *The Devil's Dictionary*

An alcoholic is someone you don't like who drinks as much as you do.

> Dylan Thomas, quoted in Constantine Fitzgibbon,
> *The Life of Dylan Thomas*

A man who exposes himself when he is intoxicated, has not the art of getting drunk.

> Samuel Johnson

Drink and dance and laugh and lie,
Love, the reeling midnight through,
For tomorrow we shall die!
(But, alas, we never do.)

> Dorothy Parker, *The Flaw in Paganism*

I am as sober as a judge.

> Henry Fielding, *Don Quixote in England*

I drink to forget I drink.

> Joe E. Lewis

I am sparkling; *you* are unusually talkative; *he* is drunk.

> *New Statesman* competition entry

Work is the curse of the drinking classes.

Anon.

Drink spoils a man for this life and ruins him for the heaven which is to come. No wonder God and the Church are fighting King Alcohol so desperately, that they are bent on his destruction. It looks now as though only five or six years of his miserable, murderous misrule will be tolerated, and that then the votes of the people will have given us a stainless flag and a saloonless nation.

Ferdinand C. Iglehart, *King Alcohol Dethroned* (1917)

But I'm not so think as you drunk I am.

J.C. Squire, *Ballade of the Glandular Hypothesis*

If I were a cassowary
On the plains of Timbuctoo,
I would eat a missionary,
Cassock, band, and hymn-book too.

Attributed to Bishop Samuel Wilberforce

Eating people is wrong.

Michael Flanders, 'The Reluctant Cannibal'

Marylebone Cricket Club
Lord's Ground
London N.W.8

Dear Mrs Peach,

It is my unhappy lot as President of the Marylebone Cricket Club to inform you that while representing the Club in New Guinea, your husband Peach, L.B., was killed and, not to beat about the bush, eaten by natives. Until the rest of the team returns to this country, I am afraid that the facts surrounding the incident needs must be rather sketchy. Suffice it to say, he was a professional, and knew what to expect. It may somewhat soften the blow to report that he had scored a most solid 38 not out prior to lunch, and there is no doubt that, had he survived that interval, he would have gone on to even better things in the afternoon session.

Needless to say, The Marylebone Cricket Club will be sending no more representative teams to New Guinea until there is firm evidence that they have changed their ways. Cannibalism, as such, is not on.

The whole Committee joins me in saying how sorry we are about poor Peach. I wonder if his name excited the gastric juices of the local team; we may never know.

Enclosed you will find a Postal Order for £3. A little something you will gather has been added to his salary for the tour, in spite of the fact that technically he did not complete it.

Yours sincerely, Sir Rambo Legge-Brake

William Rushton, *Marylebone versus The World*

I came across a tribe of cannibals who'd been converted by Roman Catholic missionaries. Now, on Friday, they only eat fishermen.

Max Kauffmann

Poor soul, very sad; her late husband, you know, a very sad death – eaten by missionaries – poor soul!

William Archibald Spooner

These citizens are always willing to bet that what Nicely-Nicely dies of will be over-feeding and never anything small like pneumonia, for Nicely-Nicely is known far and wide as a character who dearly loves to commit eating.

Damon Runyon, *Take It Easy*

Mr —, who loved buttered muffins, but durst not eat them because they disagreed with his stomach, resolved to shoot himself; and then he ate three buttered muffins for breakfast, before shooting himself, knowing that he should not be troubled with indigestion.

Topham Beauclerk, quoted in Boswell, *The Life of Samuel Johnson*

I am convinced digestion is the great secret of life.

Reverend Sydney Smith, letter to Arthur Kinglake

Smith's idea of heaven is eating pâtés de foie gras to the sound of trumpets.

H. Pearson, *The Smith of Smiths*

To eat is human; to digest, divine.

Mark Twain

Avarice

The silver dropsy

THE MISER who gets his comeuppance has a dishonourable but central role in literature. Silas Marner, Scrooge, Volpone, Shylock and Molière's Harpagon are all unforgettable figures. More often than not the miser learns his lesson, and sometimes even achieves redemption, but not before we have winced or laughed at his affliction. There is generally something faintly endearing about the depiction of even the most sordid miser. At least he loves something; and his love, however misplaced, can encompass some admirable qualities, however misdirected. Juvenal thinks him insane, but clearly Hume and Balzac, at least, have more than a sneaking regard for the obsession.

———◆———

The love of money is the root of all evil.

1 Timothy, VI.10

O cursed lust of gold! when, for thy sake,
The fool throws up his interest in both worlds,
First starved in this, then damned in that to come.

Robert Blair, *The Grave*

There is some ill a-brewing towards my rest,
For I did dream of money-bags tonight.

William Shakespeare, *The Merchant of Venice*

Sick of the silver dropsy.

John Clarke, *Paroemiologia*

Avarice and charity betray themselves by similar results; does not charity lay up in Heaven the treasure that the miser hoards on earth?

Honoré de Balzac, *Ursule Mirouët*

Much will have more.

Ralph Waldo Emerson, *Society and Solitude*

But what is the point of amassing wealth through these painful
    rigours?
Isn't it utter folly, isn't it obvious madness
To live like a beggar in order to die like a millionaire?

Juvenal, *Satires*

Shrouds have no pockets.

Jewish proverb

So, year after year, Silas Marner had lived in this solitude, his guineas rising in the iron pot, and his life narrowing and hardening itself more and more into a mere pulsation of desire and satisfaction that had no relation to any other being. His life had reduced itself to the functions of weaving and hoarding, without any contemplation of an end towards which the functions tended . . .

. . . But at night came his revelry: at night he closed his shutters, and made fast his doors, and drew forth his gold. Long ago the heap of coins had become too large for the iron pot to hold them, and he had made for them two thick leather bags, which wasted no room in their resting place, but lent themselves flexibly to every corner. How the guineas shone as they came pouring out of the dark leather mouth! The silver bore no large proportion in amount to the gold, because the long pieces of linen which formed his chief work were always partly paid for in gold, and out of the silver he supplied his own bodily wants, choosing always the shillings and sixpences to spend in this way.

He loved the guineas best, but he would not change the silver – the crowns and half-crowns that were his own earnings, begotten by his labour; he loved them all. He spread them out in heaps and bathed his hands in them; then he counted them and set them up in regular piles, and felt their rounded outline between his thumb and fingers, and thought fondly of the guineas that were only half earned by the work in his loom, as if they had been unborn children – thought of the guineas that were coming slowly through the coming years, through all his life, which spread far away before him, the end quite hidden by countless days of weaving.

George Eliot, *Silas Marner*

Good morning to the day: and next, my gold! –
Open the shrine that I may see my saint.

Ben Jonson, *Volpone*

Hoards after hoards his rising raptures fill;
Yet still he sighs, for hoards are wanting still.

Oliver Goldsmith, 'The Traveller'

He was always ready to pick a halfpenny out of the dirt with
his teeth.

Petronius, *Satyricon*

An old miser kept a tame jackdaw, that used to steal pieces of
money, and hide them in a hole, which a cat observing, asked,
'Why he would hoard up those round shining things that he
could make no use of?' 'Why,' said the jackdaw, 'my master has
a whole chest-full, and makes no more use of them than I do.'

Jonathan Swift, *Thoughts on Various Subjects*

Oh dear, my dear, darling money, my beloved, they've taken
you away from me and now you are gone I have lost my
strength, my joy and my consolation. It's all over with me.
There's nothing left for me to do in the world. I can't go on
living without you. It's the finish. I can't bear any more. I'm

dying; I'm dead – and buried. Will nobody bring me to life again by giving me my beloved money back or telling me who has taken it? Eh? What d'ye say? There's nobody there! Whoever did it must have watched his opportunity well and chosen the very moment I was talking to my blackguard of a son. I must go. I'll demand justice. I'll have everyone in the house put to the torture, menservants, maidservants, son, daughter, everyone – myself included.

Molière, *L'Avare*

My daughter! O my ducats! O my daughter!
Fled with a Christian! O my Christian ducats!
Justice! the law! my ducats, and my daughter!

William Shakespeare, *The Merchant of Venice*

What a rare punishment
Is avarice to itself!

Ben Jonson, *Volpone*

Oh! but he was a tight-fisted hand at the grindstone, Scrooge! a squeezing, wrenching, grasping, scraping, clutching, covetous old sinner! Hard and sharp as flint, from which no steel had ever struck out generous fire; secret, and self-contained, and solitary as an oyster. The cold within him froze his old features, nipped his pointed nose, shrivelled his cheek, stiffened his gait; made his eyes red, his thin lips blue; and spoke out shrewdly in his grating voice. A frosty rime was on his head, and on his eyebrows, and his wiry chin. He carried his own low temperature always about with him; he iced his coffee in the dog-days, and didn't thaw it one degree at Christmas.

External heat and cold had little influence on Scrooge. No warmth could warm, no wintry weather chill him. No wind that blew was bitterer than he, no falling snow was more intent upon its purpose, no pelting rain less open to entreaty.

Charles Dickens, *A Christmas Carol*

Economy: cutting down on other people's wages.

J.B. Morton ('Beachcomber')

Of great riches there is no real use, except it be in the distribution.

Francis Bacon, *Of Riches*

When avarice has an end in view, it ceases to be a vice; it is the instrument of virtue; its stern privations become a constant sacrifice; in short, it has greatness of purpose concealed beneath its meanness.

Honoré de Balzac, *Béatrix*

Robber: Don't make a move, this is a stick-up!

Benny: What?

Robber: You heard me.

Benny: Mister . . . Mister, put down that gun.

Robber: Shut up . . . now, come on . . . your money or your life . . . [Long pause] . . . Look bud, I said, 'Your money or your life.'

Benny: I'm thinking it over!

Jack Benny, *The Jack Benny Show*

A gold rush is what happens when a line of chorus girls spot a man with a bank roll.

Mae West, *Klondike Annie*

She felt justified in getting anything at all back that she could, money or anything else, as if she had once owned the earth and been dispossessed of it. She couldn't look at anything steadily without wanting it, and what provoked her most was the thought that there might be something valuable hidden near her, something she couldn't see.

Flannery O'Connor, *Wise Blood*

A son might bear with composure the death of his father, but the loss of his inheritance might drive him to despair.

Niccolo Machiavelli, *The Prince*

each generation wastes a little more
of the future with greed and lust for riches

Don Marquis, *archy and mehitabel*

Money, thou bane of blisse, and sourse of wo,
  Whence com'st thou, that thou art so fresh and fine?
  I know thy parentage is base and low:
Man found thee poore and dirtie in a mine.

Surely thou didst so little contribute
  To this great kingdome, which thou now hast got,
  That he was fain, when thou wert destitute,
To digge thee out of thy dark cave and grot:

Then forcing thee, by fire he made thee bright:
  Nay, thou hast got the face of man; for we
  Have with our stamp and seal transferr'd our right:
Thou art the man, and man but drosse to thee.

  Man calleth thee his wealth, who made thee rich;
  And while he digs out thee, falls in the ditch.

George Herbert, 'Avarice'

To be clever enough to get all that money, one must be stupid
enough to want it.

G.K. Chesterton, *The Innocence of Father Brown*

I'm tired of Love: I'm still more tired of Rhyme.
But Money gives me pleasure all the time.

> Hilaire Belloc, *Fatigue*

So for a good old-gentlemanly vice,
I think I must take up with avarice.

> Lord Byron, *Don Juan*

I am rich beyond the dreams of avarice.

> Edward Moore, *The Gamester*

When the paupers start dancing, the musicians stop playing.

> Jewish proverb

There is nothing so habit-forming as money.

> Don Marquis

Avarice, the spur of industry, is so obstinate a passion, and
works its way through so many real dangers and difficulties,
that it is not likely to be scared by an imaginary danger, which
is so small that it scarcely admits of calculation.

> David Hume, 'Of Civil Liberty'

There was no one in Saumur who was not convinced that
Monsieur Grandet had somewhere a private hoard, a secret
hiding place crammed with louis; it was believed that night after
night he indulged himself in the ineffable joy of looking at his
great heap of gold. Other misers in the town felt a distinct
certainty about this whenever they caught the glitter of the
yellow metal in the old man's eye. The gaze of any man
accustomed to drawing immense interest from his wealth
inevitably acquires – like the eyes of the libertine, the gambler,
or the courtier – certain indefinable habits, a greedy, furtive,
mysterious flicker; and this is not lost upon his fellow
worshippers. It is a secret language constituting in some
respects a freemasonry of the passions.

    … Financially speaking, Monsieur Grandet was a
combination of tiger and boa constrictor: he was capable of
lying hidden in wait, contemplating his prey for a long while
before pouncing. Then, when ready, he would open the jaws of
his purse, swallow a sumptuous meal of golden crowns, and
subside quietly once more, like the serpent digesting: impassive,
cold, methodical.

Honoré de Balzac, Eugénie Grandet

Mr Henry Ford
Had a little secret hoard
To which he would add a dime
From time to time.

E. Clerihew Bentley

Lust

This brutish passion

'WHILE there's life there's hope,' someone remarked, to which a cynic might add, 'And while there's lust there's life.'

Now I'm really alive, thinks the adolescent, on discovering this roller-coaster of sensation (which of course no one else has fully experienced before). And while lust is content to go hand in hand with romance, it can often seem to be the very stuff of life; when it is not, it may seem more like a disease. Even if it's a problem, however, lust has its satisfactory aspects. For as long as lust is on the scene, taking centre stage or lurking in the wings, the sufferer feels full of vitality: 'There's life in the old dog yet.' When it is no longer a factor, survivors enjoy a sense of relief that such a persistent distraction is out of the way. Or so they say.

Violent acts apart, the twentieth century has proved remarkably tolerant of lust, which is why this stormy section ranges not only from passionate adolescents to dirty old men – and women – but also from dire warnings to shameless boasting.

———◆———

Love indeed (I may not deny) first united provinces, built cities, and by a perpetual generation makes and preserves mankind; but if it rage it is no more love, but burning lust, a disease, frenzy, madness, hell…It subverts kingdoms, overthrows cities, towns, families; mars, corrupts, and makes a massacre of men; thunder and lightning, wars, fires, plagues, have not done that mischief to mankind, as this burning lust, this brutish passion.

Robert Burton, *Anatomy of Melancholy*

Whosoever looketh on a woman to lust after hath
committed adultery with her in his heart.

Matthew V.28

For men have ever a likerous appetite
On lower thing to perform their delight
Than on their wives, be they never so fair,
Nor never so true, nor so debonair.
Flesh is so newfangel, with mischaunce,
That we can in no thing have plesaunce
That tendeth unto virtue any while.

Geoffrey Chaucer, *The Manciple's Tale*

Let not his hand within your bosom stray,
And rudely with your pretty bubbies play.

John Dryden, *Imitations of Ovid: Amores*

Love comforteth like sunshine after rain,
But Lust's effect is tempest after sun;
Love's gentle spring doth always fresh remain,
Lust's winter comes ere summer half be done:
  Love surfeits not. Lust like a glutton dies;
  Love is all truth, Lust full of forged lies.

William Shakespeare, *Venus and Adonis*

Love is the answer, but while you are waiting for the answer,
sex raises some pretty good questions.

Woody Allen

Th' expence of spirit in a waste of shame
Is lust in action; and, till action, lust
Is perjured, murd'rous, bloody, full of blame,
Savage, extreme, rude, cruel, not to trust;
Enjoyed no sooner but despised straight;
Past reason hunted, and no sooner had,
Past reason hated as a swallowed bait
On purpose laid to make the taker mad;
Made in pursuit, and in possession so;
Had, having, and in quest to have, extreme;
A bliss in proof, and proved, a very woe,
Before, a joy proposed; behind, a dream.
All this the world well knows, yet none knows well
To shun the heaven that leads men to this hell.

William Shakespeare, *Sonnet CXXIX*

Love finds an altar for forbidden fires.

Alexander Pope, *Eloisa to Abelard*

Eros shakes my senses like a wind shaking the oaks.

Sappho

Eros is the youngest of the gods. He is also the most tired.

Natalie Barney

Never to be forgotten, that first long secret drink of golden fire, juice of those valleys and of that time, wine of wild orchards, of russet summer, of plump red apples, and Rosie's burning cheeks. Never to be forgotten, or ever tasted again . . .

I put down the jar with a gulp and a gasp. Then I turned to look at Rosie. She was yellow and dusty with buttercups and seemed to be purring in the gloom; her hair was rich as a wild bee's nest and her eyes were full of stings. I did not know what to do about her, nor did I know what not to do. She looked smooth and precious, a thing of unplumbable mysteries, and perilous as quicksand.

'Rosie . . .' I said, on my knees, and shaking.

She crawled with a rustle of grass towards me, quick and superbly assured. Her hand in mine was like a small wet flame which I could neither hold nor throw away. Then Rosie, with a remorseless, reedy strength, pulled me down from my tottering perch, pulled me down, down into her wide green smile and into the deep subaqueous grass.

Laurie Lee, *Cider with Rosie*

Red hair she had and golden skin,
Her sulky lips were shaped for sin.

John Betjeman, 'The Licorice Fields at Pontefract'

By the witchcraft of a cunning kiss
Has she disarmed him.

Christopher Marlowe, *Lust's Dominion*

He loved a wench well; and one time getting one of the Maids
of Honour up against a tree in a wood ('twas his first lady) who
seemed at first boarding to be something fearful of her honour,
and modest, she cried, 'Sweet Sir Walter, what do you me ask?
Will you undo me? Nay, sweet Sir Walter! Sweet Sir Walter!
Sir Walter!' At last, as the danger and the pleasure at the same
time grew higher, she cried in the ecstasy, 'Swisser Swatter,
Swisser Swatter!' She proved with child, and I doubt not but
this hero took care of them both, as also that the product was
more than an ordinary mortal.

John Aubrey, *Brief Lives*

It had a kind of charm I don't think I've ever experienced
before. Once she'd surrendered, she behaved with perfect
candour. Total mutual delirium: which for the first time ever
with me outlasted the pleasure itself. She was astonishing. So
much so that I ended by falling on my knees and pledging her
eternal love. And do you know, at the time, and for several
hours afterwards, I actually meant it!

Christopher Hampton, *Les Liaisons Dangereuses* (after Laclos)

There's no bottom, none,
In my voluptuousness: your wives, your daughters,
Your matrons and your maids, could not fill up
The cistern of my lust.

William Shakespeare, *Macbeth*

He had tasted the sweets of the flesh like a crotchety invalid
with a craving for food but a palate which soon becomes jaded.
In the days when he had belonged to a set of young men-about-
town, he had gone to those unconventional supper-parties
where drunken women loosen their dresses at dessert and beat
the table with their heads; he had hung around stage-doors, had
bedded with singers and actresses, had endured, over and
above the innate stupidity of the sex, the hysterical vanity
common to women of the theatre. Then he had kept mistresses
already famed for their depravity, and helped to swell the funds
of those agencies which supply dubious pleasures for a
consideration. And finally, weary to the point of satiety of these
hackneyed luxuries, these commonplace caresses, he had
sought satisfaction in the gutter, hoping that the contrast would
revive his exhausted desires and imagining that the fascinating
filthiness of the poor would stimulate his flagging senses.

Try what he might, however, he could not shake off the over-
powering tedium which weighed upon him.

J.-K. Huysmans, *A Rebours*

'Madam,' cries Joseph, 'I hope your ladyship will not be offended at my asserting my innocence; for by all that is sacred, I have never offered more than kissing.' 'Kissing!' said the lady, with great discomposure of countenance, and more redness in her cheeks, than anger in her eyes; 'Do you call that no crime? Kissing, Joseph, is as a prologue to a play. Can I believe a young fellow of your age and complexion will be content with kissing? No, Joseph, there is no woman who grants that, but will grant more; and I am deceived greatly in you, if you would not put her closely to it. What would you think, Joseph, if I admitted you to kiss me?' Joseph replied, He would sooner die than have any such thought. 'And yet, Joseph,' returned she, 'ladies have admitted their footmen to such familiarities; and footmen, I confess to you, much less deserving them; fellows without half your charms . . .'

Henry Fielding, *Joseph Andrews*

To set your neighbour's bed a-shaking is now an ancient and long-established custom. It was the silver age that saw the first adulterers.

Juvenal, *Satires*

So heavy is the chain of wedlock that it needs two to carry it, and sometimes three.

Alexandre Dumas

What men call gallantry, and gods adultery,
Is much more common where the climate's sultry.

Lord Byron, *Don Juan*

It is better to love two too many than one too few.

Sir John Harington

What was thy cause? Adultery?
Thou shalt not die: die for adultery? No!
The wren goes to't, and the small gilded fly
Does lecher in my sight. Let copulation thrive.

William Shakespeare, *King Lear*

Ladies are one emotion, and guys detached. Not consciously detached, but they just do detach. Like, a lady can't go through a plate glass window and go to bed with you five seconds later. But every guy in this audience is the same – you can *idolize* your wife, just be so crazy about her, be on the way home from work, have a head-on collision with a Greyhound bus, in a *disaster* area. Forty people laying dead on the highway – not even in the hospital, in the *ambulance* – the guy makes a play for the nurse . . .

Lenny Bruce, *The Essential Lenny Bruce*

If the girls at a Yale weekend were laid end to end I wouldn't be a bit surprised.

Dorothy Parker

What is a promiscuous person? It's usually someone who is getting more sex than you are.

Victor Lownes

Would you like to sin
With Elinor Glyn
On a tiger skin?
Or would you prefer
To err
With her
On some other fur?

Anon.

Lolita, light of my life, fire of my loins. My sin, my soul. Lo-lee-ta: the tip of the tongue taking a trip of three steps down the palate to tap, at three, on the teeth. Lo. Lee. Ta.

She was Lo, plain Lo, in the morning, standing four feet ten in one sock. She was Lola in slacks. She was Dolly at school. She was Dolores on the dotted line. But in my arms she was always Lolita.

Vladimir Nabokov, *Lolita*

I wasn't kissing her – I was whispering in her mouth.

Chico Marx, on being caught by his wife dallying with a chorus girl

Dancing is a perpendicular expression of a horizontal desire.

Anon.

The pleasure is momentary, the position is ridiculous, and the expense damnable.

Lord Chesterfield

Unless you happen to live in one of those delightfully backward Latin countries where husbands are encouraged to form liaisons with other women instead of loitering round the house and watching TV, the mistress is forbidden fruit. She is a threat to the fabric of polite society, a wrecker of homes and a walking distraction to men who should be keeping their eye on the corporate ball. She wears black underwear. She takes long, scented baths. She sneers at housework. She is either feared or envied, or both, by fifty per cent of the married population of America. She is illicit . . . If mistresses were socially acceptable, they would lose much of their appeal; it is the whiff of sin and the fear of discovery that sharpen the pleasure, make parting such sweet sorrow and enable a man to contemplate his American Express bills with a secret smile.

Peter Mayle, *Expensive Habits*

Sex is dangerous – it's a dangerous sport.

Camille Paglia, *Sex, Art, and American Culture*

Sex is a body-contact sport. It is safe to watch but more fun to play.

Thomas Szasz, *Sex by Prescription*

Sex is the great amateur sport. The professional, male or female, is frowned upon; he or she misses the whole point and spoils the show.

David Cort, *Social Astonishments*

To err is human – but it feels divine.

Mae West

When I'm good I'm very very good, but when I'm bad I'm better.

Mae West

A man is as young as the woman he feels.

Groucho Marx

Give a man a free hand and he'll run it all over you.

Mae West

Men are creatures with two legs and eight hands.

Jayne Mansfield

Anon: Goodness, what beautiful diamonds!
Mae West: Goodness had nothing to do with it, dearie.

Night After Night

Anon: Is sex dirty?
Woody Allen: Only if it's done right.

All You Ever Wanted to Know about Sex

Hogamous, higamous
Man is polygamous
Higamous, hogamous
Woman monogamous.

William James

Envy

A coal hissing hot from hell

ENVY is nobody's favourite sin. Unlike the others, as Angus Wilson and Robert Burton agree, it has no redeeming feature. Even from a literary point of view, envy has less to recommend it than the other sins. It has, of course, played an important and corrosive role in novels and plays, most spectacularly in *Othello*, where Iago's envy and Othello's jealousy combine to undo everyone. At the lighter end of the spectrum, however, perhaps because Invidia is such an unattractive, mean-spirited character, there seem to be fewer *bons mots* and entertaining poems on her than on her deadly companions. I have therefore given her less space here than most of them, which will doubt-less cause her further unhappiness.

And in process of time it came to pass, that Cain brought of the fruit of the ground an offering unto the Lord.

And Abel, he also brought of the firstlings of his flock and of the fat thereof. And the Lord had respect unto Abel and to his offering:

But unto Cain and to his offering he had not respect. And Cain was very wroth, and his countenance fell.

Genesis, IV.3–5

The grass is always greener on the other side of the fence.

English proverb

Thou shalt not covet thy neighbour's house, thou shalt not
covet thy neighbour's wife, nor his manservant, nor his
maidservant, nor his ox, nor his ass, nor any thing that is thy
neighbour's.

Exodus XX.17

All the seven deadly sins are self-destroying, morbid appetites,
but in their early stages at least, lust and gluttony, avarice and
sloth know some gratification, while anger and pride have
power, even though that power eventually destroys it. Envy is
impotent, numbed with fear, never ceasing in its appetite, and
it knows no gratification, but endless self torment. It has the
ugliness of a trapped rat, which gnaws its own foot in an effort
to escape.

Angus Wilson, *The Sunday Times*

Every other sin hath some pleasure annexed to it, or will admit
of some excuse; but envy wants both.

Robert Burton, *Anatomy of Melancholy*

Jealousy is in some measure just and reasonable, since it
merely aims at keeping something that belongs to us or we
think belongs to us, whereas envy is a frenzy that cannot bear
anything that belongs to others.

La Rochefoucauld, *Maxims*

Roderigo: Thou told'st me thou didst hold him in thy hate.

Iago: Despise me if I do not. Three great ones of the city,
In personal suit to make me his lieutenant,
Off-capp'd to him; and, by the faith of man,
I know my price, I am worth no worse a place;
But he, as loving his own pride and purposes,
Evades them, with a bombast circumstance
Horribly stuff'd with epithets of war;
And, in conclusion,
Nonsuits my mediators; for, 'Certes,' says he,
'I have already chose my officer.'
And what was he?
Forsooth, a great arithmetician,
One Michael Cassio, a Florentine,
A fellow almost damn'd in a fair wife;
That never set a squadron in the field,
Nor the division of a battle knows
More than a spinster; unless the bookish theoric,
Wherein the toged consuls can propose
As masterly as he: mere prattle, without practice,
Is all his soldiership. But he, sir, had the election;
And I, of whom his eyes had seen the proof
At Rhodes, at Cyprus, and on other grounds
Christian and heathen, must be be-lee'd and calm'd
By debitor and creditor, this counter-caster;
He, in good time, must his lieutenant be,
And I, God bless the mark! his Moorship's ancient.

William Shakespeare, *Othello*

The infernal serpent; he it was, whose guile,
Stirred up with envy and revenge, deceived
The mother of mankind.

John Milton, *Paradise Lost*

Envy's a coal comes hissing hot from hell.

Philip James Bailey, *Festus*

Some men do as much begrudge others a good name as they
want one themselves; and perhaps that is the reason of it.

William Penn, *Reflexions and Maxims*

Base envy withers at another's joy,
And hates the excellence it cannot reach.

James Thomson, *The Seasons*

Envy with its crooked fingers and its pale, livid face.

P.A.C. de Beaumarchais, *Le Barbier de Seville*

Wrath killeth the foolish man, and envy slayeth the silly one.

Job, V.2

The angels, not half so happy in heaven,
  Went envying her and me –
Yes! – that was the reason (as all men know,
  In this kingdom by the sea)
That the wind came out of the cloud by night,
  Chilling and killing my Annabel Lee . . .

Edgar Allan Poe, 'Annabel Lee'

Calamities are of two kinds: misfortune to ourselves and good fortune to others.

Ambrose Bierce, *The Devil's Dictionary*

He was a man of strong passions, and the green-eyed monster ran up his leg and bit him to the bone.

P.G. Wodehouse, *Full Moon*

A show of envy is an insult to oneself.

Yevgeny Yevtushenko

I believe now that I was exposed too early to goodness and that I never recovered.

Trapped in the fierce grasp of Elizabeth's kindness, aware constantly of the truthfulness of her gaze, I suffocated on the high thinness of the air around her. The corrosive power of her generosity killed, as they rose in me, my own small instincts towards goodness.

. . . Encouraged when small to follow the sweetness of her behaviour – to imitate her many acts of generosity, to note her kindness – I followed in cold envy the path she laid before me through the years. Like Satan before the Fall, I came to hate the very nature of goodness, to fear its power.

But during childhood I lacked the courage for rebellion. So I went underground. To search for secret ways to be. And secret ways to lessen her.

Josephine Hart, *Sin*

Anybody can sympathize with the sufferings of a friend, but it requires a very fine nature to sympathize with a friend's success.

Oscar Wilde, 'The Soul of Man under Socialism'

Some folks rail against other folks because other folks have what some folks would be glad of.

Henry Fielding, *Joseph Andrews*

He is less upset by his poverty than your wealth.

Jewish saying

The man with toothache thinks everyone happy whose teeth are sound.

George Bernard Shaw, *Man and Superman*

There is not a passion so strongly rooted in the human heart as envy.

R.B. Sheridan, *The Critic*

There is a strong disposition in youth, from which some individuals never escape, to suppose that everyone else is having a more enjoyable time than we are ourselves.

Anthony Powell, *A Buyer's Market*

Just as the body contracts diseases, the soul contracts the canker of envy. In little natures envy becomes a base and brutal covetousness, shrinking from sight, but from nothing else; in cultivated minds it fosters subversive doctrines, which a man uses as a stepping-stone to raise himself above his superiors.

Honoré de Balzac, *Les Paysans*

Envy is the sincerest form of flattery.

Churton Collins, *Aphorisms*

The dullard's envy of brilliant men is always assuaged by the suspicion that they will come to a bad end.

Max Beerbohm, *Zuleika Dobson*

In a consumer society there are inevitably two kinds of slaves: the prisoners of addiction and the prisoners of envy.

Ivan Illich, *Tools for Conviviality*

Envy is the basis of democracy.

Bertrand Russell, *Conquest of Happiness*

The rich man has his motorcar,
His country and his town estate.
He smokes a fifty-cent cigar
And jeers at Fate.
He frivols through the livelong day,
He knows not poverty her pinch.
His lot seems light, his heart seems gay,
He has a cinch.
Yet though my lamp burns low and dim,
Though I must slave for livelihood –
Think you that I would change with him?
You bet I would!

Franklin P. Adams, *By and Large*

To proclaim the equality of all is to declare the rights of the envious.

Honoré de Balzac, *Béatrix*

This only grant me, that my means may lie
Too low for envy, for contempt too high.

Abraham Cowley, 'Of Myself'

I go about looking at horses and cattle. They eat grass, make love, work when they have to, bear their young. I am sick with envy of them.

Sherwood Anderson, *Letters*

Pride

The self-regarding gaze

'SIR, ever since the dark days before Pearl Harbor I have been proud to wear this uniform . . . ' So begins the ever handy resignation speech routinely offered at every setback by the commanding officer of the surgical unit in *M.A.S.H.*, Robert Altman's Korean War comedy. Sure enough, we are now expected to say we are proud of our children, our gardens, our colleges, our regiments, our countries . . . ourselves. Teams are told to play with passion and pride, and congratulate themselves when they do so. However unpleasant a spectacle this may be, pride is apparently no longer anything to be ashamed of. Quite the opposite – it is something to be proud of. Meanwhile it is no doubt true to say that personal pride has also played its part in many outstanding feats of courage and endurance.

The sin examined in the following pages still exists of course, but now we think of it in terms of conceit, vanity, egotism and, more especially, arrogance – 'an haughty spirit'. Even so, when the most insufferable haughtiness is paraded by the likes of Oscar Wilde or James McNeill Whistler, we tend to suffer it quite gladly. (I can't help adding that I am particularly pleased with the way this chapter has turned out.)

Pride goeth before destruction, and an haughty spirit before a fall.

Book of Proverbs

The tyrant is a child of Pride
Who drinks from his great sickening cup
Recklessness and vanity,
Until from his high crest headlong
He plummets to the dust of hope.

Sophocles, *Oedipus Rex*

Pride is the reservoir of sin.

Ben Sirach, *Ecclesiasticus*

Of all the causes which conspire to blind
Man's erring judgement, and misguide the mind,
What the weak head with strongest bias rules,
Is Pride, the never-failing vice of fools.

Alexander Pope, *An Essay on Criticism*

I will not be interrupted! Hear me in silence. My daughter and my nephew are formed for each other. They are descended on the maternal side, from the same noble line; and, on the father's, from respectable, honourable, and ancient, though untitled families. Their fortune on both sides is splendid. They are destined for each other by the voice of every member of their respective houses; and what is to divide them? – the upstart pretensions of a young woman without family, connections, or fortune. Is this to be endured! But it must not, shall not be!

If you were sensible of your own good, you would not wish to quit the sphere in which you have been brought up.

Jane Austen, *Pride and Prejudice*

Some glory in their birth, some in their skill,
Some in their wealth, some in their bodies' force,
Some in their garments, though new-fangled ill;
Some in their hawks and hounds, some in their horse;
And every humour hath his adjunct pleasure,
Wherein it finds a joy above the rest.

William Shakespeare, *Sonnet XCI*

Pride is therefore pleasure arising from a man's thinking too highly of himself.

Benedict Spinoza, *Ethics*

He fell in love with himself at first sight and it is a passion to which he has always remained faithful. Self-love seems so often unrequited.

Anthony Powell, *The Acceptance World*

To love oneself is the beginning of a lifelong romance.

Oscar Wilde, 'Phrases and Philosophies for the Use of the Young'

Conceit is the finest armour a man can wear.

Jerome K. Jerome, *Idle Thoughts of an Idle Fellow*

I never knew a mocker who was not mocked . . . a deceiver who was not deceived, or a proud man who was not humbled.

Marguerite of Navarre, *The Heptameron*

The truly proud man knows neither superiors nor inferiors. The first he does not admit of: the last he does not concern himself about.

William Hazlitt, *Characteristics*

There are few who would not rather be taken in adultery than in provincialism.

Aldous Huxley, *Antic Hay*

Certainly, there is nothing else here to enjoy.

George Bernard Shaw, to the hostess at a party,
who asked him whether he was enjoying himself

I've never any pity for conceited people, because I think they carry their comfort about them.

George Eliot, *The Mill on the Floss*

What makes the vanity of other people insupportable is that it wounds our own.

La Rochefoucauld, *Maxims*

Egotist, *n.* A person of low taste, more interested in himself than in me.

Ambrose Bierce, *The Devil's Dictionary*

Is it against reason or justice to love ourselves? And why is self-love always a vice?

Marquis de Vauvenargues, *Réflexions et Maximes*

Whoever desires the character of a proud man ought to conceal his vanity.

Jonathan Swift, *Thoughts on Various Subjects*

I explained to him I had simple tastes and didn't want anything ostentatious, no matter what it cost me.

Art Buchwald, 'A New Lease on Texas'

Though pride is not a virtue, it is the parent of many virtues.

Churton Collins, *Aphorisms*

The perfection preached in the Gospels never yet built up an empire. Every man of action has a strong dose of egotism, pride, hardness, and cunning. But all those things will be forgiven him, indeed, they will be regarded as high qualities, if he can make of them the means to achieve great ends.

Charles de Gaulle, *Le Fil de l'Epée*

In peace there's nothing so becomes a man
As modest stillness and humility.

William Shakespeare, *Henry V*

It is difficult to be humble. Even if you aim at humility, there is no guarantee that when you have attained the state you will not be proud of the feat.

Bonamy Dobree, *John Wesley*

A confessional passage has probably never been written that didn't stink a little bit of the writer's pride in having given up his pride.

J.D. Salinger, *Seymour: an Introduction*

There is false modesty, but there is no false pride.

Jules Renard, *Journal*

Godolphin Horne was Nobly Born;
He held the Human Race in Scorn,
And lived with all his Sisters where
His Father lived, in Berkeley Square.
And oh! the Lad was Deathly Proud!
He never shook your Hand or Bowed,
But merely smirked and nodded thus:
How perfectly ridiculous!
Alas! That such Affected Tricks
Should flourish in a Child of Six!

Hilaire Belloc, *Cautionary Tales for Children*

Although, looking back, I can see that my parents let me down badly in almost every department throughout my young life, I bear no grudge. Raising a gifted child is never easy, even for a normal couple. For Mother and Father, it turned out to be impossible.

Terence Blacker, *Fixx*

Charity, dear Miss Prism, charity! None of us are perfect. I myself am peculiarly susceptible to draughts.

Oscar Wilde, *The Importance of Being Earnest*

When you're as great as I am, it's hard to be humble.

Muhammad Ali

What the world needs is more geniuses with humility. There are
so few of us left.

Oscar Levant

I apologize
For boasting, but once you know my qualities
I can drop back into a quite brilliant
Humility.

Christopher Fry, *The Lady's Not for Burning*

And the Devil did grin, for his darling sin
Is pride that apes humility.

S.T. Coleridge, 'The Devil's Thoughts'

The nymph still looks at herself and admires herself in the
water, as she has done since the beginning of time. Long before
Hubris entered Arcadia, the terrible intoxication was known.
The gravest crimes, the most senseless adventures have sprung
from the self-regarding gaze, and though we make poetry of
pride in the West, and pretend to ourselves that there are some
forms of pride which are legitimate and others which are not so,
the most deathly instrument placed in the hands of man remains
the mirror.

Robert Payne, *The Wanton Nymph*

Nothing, except my genius.

> Oscar Wilde, on being asked at US customs
> whether he had anything to declare

That he is indeed one of the very greatest masters of painting, is my opinion. And I may add that in this opinion Mr Whistler himself entirely concurs.

> Oscar Wilde, *Pall Mall Gazette*

'I only know of two painters in the world,' said a newly introduced feminine enthusiast to Whistler, 'yourself and Velasquez.' 'Why,' answered Whistler in dulcet tones, 'why drag in Velasquez?'

> D.C. Seitz, *Whistler Stories*

I'm very good at integral and differential calculus,
I know the scientific names of beings animalculus;
In short, in matters vegetable, animal, and mineral,
I am the very model of a modern major-general.

> W.S. Gilbert, *The Pirates of Penzance*

'There is very little to tell,' said Mrs Merdle, reviewing the breadth of bosom which seemed essential to her having room enough to be unfeeling in, 'but it is to your sister's credit.

I pointed out to your sister the plain state of the case; the impossibility of the Society in which we moved recognizing the Society in which she moved – though charming, I have no doubt; the immense disadvantage at which she would conse-quently place the family she had so high an opinion of, upon which we should find ourselves compelled to look down with contempt, and from which (socially speaking) we should feel obliged to recoil with abhorrence. In short, I made an appeal to that laudable pride in your sister.'

Charles Dickens, *Little Dorrit*

A pompous woman of his acquaintance, complaining that the head-waiter of a restaurant had not shown her and her husband immediately to a table, said, 'We had to tell him who we were.' Gerald [Lord Berners], interested, enquired, 'And who were you?'

Edith Sitwell, *Taken Care Of*

Faith, that's as well said, as if I had said it myself.

Jonathan Swift, *Polite Conversation*

Sloth

That shameful siren

I HAD intended to write an introductory paragraph for sloth, as for the other sins, but now it hardly seems worth it. After all, a reader who has got this far is hardly going to give up on the book just because of a missing introduction. In any case, I'm not sure that sloth is really a sin. Quite often, I think, what people call idleness is more a matter of being a bit indecisive, maybe too easygoing – or just failing to get everything together at the appropriate time – than anything deadly. Anyway, here are some pithy words on the subject and some examples of like-able slobs in literature and song.

———◆———

There are two cardinal sins from which all the others spring: impatience and laziness.

Franz Kafka, *Letters*

For sluggard's brow the laurel never grows;
Renown is not the child of indolent repose.

James Thomson, *The Castle of Indolence*

Idleness and lack of occupation tend – nay are dragged – towards evil.

Hippocrates, *Decorum*

I look upon indolence as a sort of suicide; for the man is effectually destroyed, though the appetites of the brute may survive.

Lord Chesterfield, *Letters*

Sluggish idleness, the nurse of sin.

Edmund Spenser, *The Faerie Queene*

Indolence is the sleep of the mind.

Marquis de Vauvenargues, *Réflexions et Maximes*

That shameful Siren, sloth, is ever to be avoided.

Horace, *Satires*

Our nature consists in movement; absolute rest is death.

Blaise Pascal, *Pensées*

Thee, too, my Paridel! she marked thee there,
Stretched on the rack of a too easy chair,
And heard thy everlasting yawn confess
The pains and penalties of idleness.

Alexander Pope, *The Dunciad*

Idleness is the canker of the mind.

John Bodenham, *Belvedere*

But he is weak; both Man and Boy,
Hath been an idler in the land;
Contented if he might enjoy
The things which others understand.

William Wordsworth, 'A Poet's Epitaph'

We grow old more through indolence than through age.

Christina of Sweden

The children of Lord Lytton organized a charade. The scene displayed a Crusader knight returning from the wars. At his gate he was welcomed by his wife to whom he recounted his triumphs and the number of heathen he had slain. His wife, pointing to a row of dolls of various sizes, replied with pride, 'And I too, my lord, have not been idle.'

G.W.E. Russell, *Collections and Recollections*

I must from this enchanting queen break off;
Ten thousand harms, more than the ills I know,
My idleness doth hatch.

William Shakespeare, *Antony and Cleopatra*

For Satan finds some mischief still
For idle hands to do.

Isaac Watts, *Divine Songs for Children*

The devil finds some mischief still for hands that have not learnt
how to be idle.

Geoffrey Madan, *Twelve Reflections*

I would rather entreat thy company
To see the wonders of the world abroad,
Than, living dully sluggardized at home,
Wear out thy youth with shapeless idleness.

William Shakespeare, *The Two Gentlemen of Verona*

Never do today what you can
Put off till tomorrow.

William Brighty Rands, *Lilliput Levee*

It is an undoubted truth, that the less one has to do, the less
time one finds to do it in. One yawns, one procrastinates,
one can do it when one will, and therefore one seldom does
it at all.

Lord Chesterfield, *Letters*

'You're just lazy, that's what's wrong with you. If you wasn't lazy you could haul a load every day, and I'd have me some snuff when I wanted it most.'

'I got to be thinking about farming the land,' Jeeter said. 'I ain't no durn woodchopper. I'm a farmer. Them woodchoppers hauling wood to Augusta ain't got no farming to take up their time, like I has. Why, I expect I'm going to grow near about fifty bales of cotton this year, if I can borrow the mules and get some seed-cotton and guano on credit in Fuller. By God and by Jesus, I'm a farmer. I ain't no durn woodchopper.'

'That's the way you talk every year about this time, but you don't never get started. It's been seven or eight years since you turned a furrow. I been listening to you talk about taking up farming again so long I don't believe nothing you say now. It's a big old whopping lie. All you men is like that. There's a hundred more just like you all around here, too. None of you is going to do nothing, except talk. The rest of them go around begging, but you're so lazy you won't even do that.'

'Now, Ada,' Jeeter said, 'I'm going to start in the morning . . . '

Erskine Caldwell, *Tobacco Road*

'I won't think of it now. I can't stand it if I do. I'll think of it tomorrow at Tara. Tomorrow's another day.'

Margaret Mitchell, *Gone with the Wind*

If a thing's worth doing, it's worth doing late.

Frederick Oliver

I am happiest when I am idle. I could live for months without performing any kind of labour, and at the expiration of that time I should feel fresh and vigorous enough to go right on in the same way for numerous more months.

Artemus Ward, *Pyrotechny*

One of the pleasures of reading old letters is the knowledge that they need no answer.

Lord Byron

The laziest man I ever met put popcorn in his pancakes so they would turn over by themselves.

W.C. Fields

My son has taken up meditation – at least it's better than sitting doing nothing.

Max Kauffmann

Better to have loafed and lost than never to have loafed at all.

James Thurber, *Fables for Our Time*

It is impossible to enjoy idling thoroughly unless one has plenty of work to do. There is no fun in doing nothing when you have nothing to do. Wasting time is merely an occupation then, and a most exhausting one. Idleness, like kisses, to be sweet must be stolen.

Jerome K. Jerome, *Idle Thoughts of an Idle Fellow*

Sloth in writers is always a symptom of an acute inner conflict, especially that laziness which renders them incapable of doing the thing which they are most looking forward to . . .
Perfectionists are notoriously lazy and all true artistic indolence is deeply neurotic; a pain not a pleasure.

Cyril Connolly, *Enemies of Promise*

A man is not idle because he is absorbed in thought. There is a visible labour and there is an invisible labour.

Victor Hugo, *Les Misérables*

Thought is the labour of the intellect, reverie is its pleasure.

Victor Hugo, *Les Misérables*

Perhaps man is the only being that can properly be called idle.

Samuel Johnson, *The Idler*

An inability to stay quiet, an irritable desire to act directly, is one of the most conspicuous failings of mankind.

Walter Bagehot, *Physics and Politics*

If men would think more, they would act less.

Lord Halifax, *Works*

As peace is the end of war, so to be idle is the ultimate purpose of the busy.

Samuel Johnson, *The Idler*

There is one piece of advice, in a life of study, which I think no one will object to; and that is, every now and then to be completely idle – to do nothing at all.

Sydney Smith, *Sketches of Moral Philosophy*

To spend too much time in studies is sloth.

Francis Bacon, *Essays*, 'Of Studies'

Life does not agree with philosophy: there is no happiness without idleness, and only the useless is pleasurable.

Anton Chekhov, *Note-Books*

Idleness is an appendix to nobility.

Robert Burton, *Anatomy of Melancholy*

We would all be idle if we could.

James Boswell, *Life of Johnson*

Lying down was not for Oblomov a necessity, as it is for a sick man or a man who is sleepy; or a matter of chance, as it is for a man who is tired; or a pleasure, as it is for a lazy man: it was his normal condition. When he was at home – and he was almost always at home – he lay down all the time, and always in the same room, the room in which we have found him and which served him as a bedroom, study, and reception-room. He had three more rooms, but he seldom looked into them, except perhaps in the morning, and that, too, not every day, but only when his man-servant swept his study – which did not happen every day. In those rooms the furniture was covered with dust sheets and the curtains were drawn.

Ivan Goncharov, *Oblomov*

procrastination is the
art of keeping
up with yesterday

Don Marquis, *archy and mehitabel*

That indolent but agreeable condition of doing nothing.

Pliny the Younger, *Letters*

It's not 'cause I wouldn't,
It's not 'cause I shouldn't,
And, Lord knows, it's not 'cause I couldn't,
It's simply because I'm the laziest gal in town.

'Laziest Gal in Town' (sung by Marlene Dietrich in *Stage Fright*)

I make no secret of the fact that I would rather lie on a sofa than sweep beneath it. But you have to be efficient if you are going to be lazy.

Shirley Conran, *Superwoman*

On the idle hill of summer,
  Sleepy with the flow of streams,
Far I hear the steady drummer
  Drumming like a noise in dreams.

A.E. Housman, *A Shropshire Lad*

My only hobby is laziness, which naturally rules out all the others.

Granni Nazzano

Lazybones, sleepin' in the sun,
How you 'spect to get your day's work done?
You'll never get your day's work done
Sleepin' in the noonday sun.
Lazybones, sleepin' in the shade,
How you 'spect to get your cornmeal made?
You'll never get your cornmeal made
Sleepin' in the evenin' shade.
Now when them taters need sprayin'
I bet you keep prayin'
That the bugs fall off of the vine,
And when you go fishin'
I bet you keep wishin'
That the fish won't grab at your line.
You're a lazybones,
Loafin' all the day,
How you 'spect to make a dime that way?
You'll never make a dime that way –
You never hear a word I say.
Sleepin' all the day,
You're a good-for-nothin' lazybones.

Hoagy Carmichael, 'Lazybones'

I have so much to do that I am going to bed.

Savoyard proverb